Ross Ship Series

FLAGS, FUNNELS AND HULL COLOURS

by
COLIN STEWART
Extra Master, ASSOC.I.N.A., M.I.N.

ADLARD COLES LIMITED
(Formerly Robert Ross & Co. Ltd.)
In association with
GEORGE G. HARRAP AND COMPANY LIMITED
LONDON TORONTO SYDNEY
WELLINGTON

CONTENTS

	page
Foreword and Introduction	3
House Flags and their Origins	5
The Development of a typical House Flag	7
Alphabetical Index	8
Flags, Funnels and Hull Colours. Gt. Britain—Commonwealth—U.S.A.	17
Abbreviations of Nationalities used and Colour Code	68
National Flags and Tonnages	69
Flags and Funnels. Europe—Asia—S. America	71

Copyright 1953

PRINTED IN GREAT BRITAIN
BY T. H. BRICKELL AND SON, LTD., THE BLACKMORE PRESS
GILLINGHAM, DORSET

FOREWORD AND INTRODUCTION

In SPITE of progress in air transport, the sea still remains the greatest universal trading link in the world today.

Those interested in ships, be it from a commercial viewpoint or purely for pleasure, are often puzzled by the ability of some observers to recognise a ship instantly they see her. This art has been well explained in Mr. Laurence Dunn's books on *Ship Recognition*, and the object of this little book on the colours of the *Flags, Funnels and Hulls*, is to give yet a further aid to ship recognition.

For 1952, *Lloyd's Register of Shipping* gave the total number of merchant ships of the world as 32,318, representing a gross tonnage of 90,868,495 tons—(this included about 800 ships on the Great Lakes of North America). It was manifestly impossible to give particulars of all their companies within the compass of this pocket sized volume. I have therefore devoted myself principally to the ships of the English speaking world: Great Britain, the Commonwealth and the United States of America. The flags, funnels and hull colours of over three hundred shipping companies are here presented. In addition there are one hundred and twenty four representative of the principal foreign companies and also many extras in black and white.

The pictorial display of hull colours as a means of identification, is a new feature hitherto overlooked, except in the plates appearing in Mr. Dodman's excellent "Observer's Book of Ships". The hull markings and colours of a ship are very important, for they are often more distinguishable than the house flag. Most shipping companies have definite colour schemes but there are, occasionally, slight variations depending upon the general profile form of the ship. For instance the 'spirket' plate on the foc's'le is sometimes white when the bulwark is not, and sometimes a ship may have a white midship bulwark whilst those for'd and aft are the colour of the hull.

Notwithstanding these variations, the hull colour of a ship can go a long way to establishing her identity. It is one of the five major factors in the recognition of a ship, which I place in the following order:—

    (i) Her general profile and size, and thus her type or classification.

    (ii) Her funnel markings.

    (iii) Her hull colour.

(iv) Her house flag.

(v) Her ensign, showing country of ownership.

I hope that this little volume may prove useful. Great care has been taken in its preparation and, although it has not always been possible to portray exact shades of colour by means of 4-colour line blocks, the basic colours are represented.

The problem confronting the author and publisher was to give a balanced and reasonable representation of the characteristic colours of the World's Shipping, within the limitations of a pocket sized book. There must be omissions, notably China, but Germany and Japan have their fair share of entries and many new companies of other countries have been included.

I would like to place on record my sincere thanks to all the Companies who have supplied information for this book. To Mr. J. H. Isherwood and Mr. Laurence Dunn for their advice and great assistance, and last, but not least, to my wife, who did the majority of drawings and helped with the formidable task of sorting and grouping them.

HOUSE FLAGS AND THEIR ORIGINS

It is usual, customary and correct for the house flag of a company to be worn at the mainmast head; however there are exceptions, and as Commander Hilary Mead has pointed out in his book on Sea Flags,* the Brocklebank Line have always used the foremast. Today with many single-masted ships it can only be worn at the fore, and I have seen it on the starboard yard when the foremost head has been taken by a complimentary ensign.

The story of the design of each flag would make interesting reading, especially of the older companies. Many, however, are self evident by the use of the alphabetical initials of the company upon plain coloured flags; though even these show subtleties of design. An example of this is that of the Lamport and Holt Line, who do not have an "&" between the letters "L" and "H", but a +. This is more symbolic of the personality of the line founded, in 1865, by W. J. Lamport and George Holt.

The London Scottish Lines have the arms of the City of London imposed upon the Scottish Saltire, whilst the London and Edinburgh Shipping Company carries the arms of each city on a plain white flag. A similar pattern of design is incorporated in the Irish Shipping's house flag; this is the red diagonal cross of St. Patrick with the addition of the arms of the four Provinces, one in each division of the field.

The beautiful Stag Line house flag bears the crest of the Robinson family, who founded the company in 1846.

The origin of the house flag of the Federal Steam Navigation Company is of considerable interest. In 1824 the "Sir Edward Paget", one of Money Wigram's clippers, was anchored off Spithead flying the St. George's Cross at the Main. That was and still is, the flag flown by an Admiral and so a naval pinnace was sent by an H.M. frigate to investigate. There being no admiral aboard, the Master was censured and ordered to haul down his flag, but thinking his masthead looked bare he re-hoisted the flag after a blue pocket handkerchief had been sewn on the middle of the cross.

A further interesting flag is that of the P and O (Peninsula and Orient) Steam Navigation Company. In the Portuguese Insurrection of 1832, Wilcox and Anderson, London shipowners, rendered valuable services to Queen Maria, providing ships and ammunition and helping to raise a loan in England, all at considerable financial and personal risk to the partners. Similarly, in the Carlist Insurrection in Spain, the two gave active support to the cause of Isabella, the Queen Regent. Both by Portugal and Spain these services were rewarded with valuable trading facilities, and the flag of the partners—later the P and O—commemorates this early history, the blue and white being the national colours of Portugal quartered with the red and yellow of Spain.

Sometimes a flag and a pennant are worn together, and quoting Boyd Cable, Commander Hilary Mead points out that this combination has its origin in the days of the sail era. When steam propulsion was first introduced it was not always possible to distinguish a steam from a sailing vessel because the funnel may well have been hidden by masts. To facilitate this distinction a pennant known as a "steam cornet" was hoisted in addition to the house flag. The custom survives today. In fact the burgee worn by Trinity House ships is still termed a cornet.

The origin of this double signification is undoubtedly true, but the amalgamation of two companies would also give cause for this, as with the Moss Hutchison Line.

Their fleet which runs to the Iberian peninsula wear both the old Moss Line pennant, and the tri-colour of the old J. and P. Hutchison company; their Mediterranean fleet wearing only the pennant.

The ships of the Glen Line, in which are inaugurated those of the Shire Line, wear the Glen Line house flag. The blue pennant with the white Maltese Cross being worn, according to the Company's tradition, to commemorate the Glen Line victories in the China Tea Race in 1874. Their ship *Glenartney* gained this "blue riband" with a passage time from Woosung to London in 44 days.

It is also of interest to note that each vessel of the Clan Line carries a flag on the jackstaff, at the bow of the ship, which is that of the tartan of the Clan after which the ship is named. Upon the tartan background is also the lion of the house flag.

Many other interesting facts could be brought to light, but space does not permit. The changes of design of the Orient Line house flag here illustrated, show quite clearly the origin of their house flag today —the *blue colour* of the St. George's Cross being the only remaining similarity to the original house flag of Anderson Thomson and Co.

1.

4.

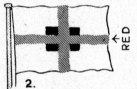

2.

5.

3.

6.

BLUE

RED

THE DEVELOPMENT OF A
TYPICAL HOUSE FLAG

1 House flag of Anderson, Anderson & Co., formerly Anderson, Thomson & Co., flown by their Orient line Clippers. 1877, first house flag flown by steamships in the joint Australian Service. Changed in 1878.

2 House flag of R. & H. Green & Co., which had become F. Green & Co when the Company joined with Andersons to form the joint Australian Service.

3 1878. Original Orient S.N. Co's. house flag, a combination of the Anderson and the Green flags. Only flown until about 1880.

4 1880 until about 1892. Similar to the Pacific Steam Navigation Co's. house flag except for their lettering, 'P S N C'.

5 About 1892 to 1908.

6 1908 to present day. The letters were dropped on the Company becoming independent of the P.S.N.C. and R.M.S.P.Co. It is now the Orient Line house flag.

7

ALPHABETICAL INDEX

Having found the number of the shipping company required, the reader should cross-check the name with the Numerical Index on the page opposite the illustrations of the company in question.

A

Aaby's, E. B., Rederi A/S	335
Aberdeen and Commonwealth Line	145
Acadia Overseas Freighters Ltd...	154
Achille Lauro Armatore	432
Adelaide Steamship Co. Ltd.	167
Admiralty	302
"Adriatica" Società per Azioni Nav.	415
Aktieselskabet Det Ostasiatiske Komp...	376
Alaska Steamship Co.	191
Albyn Line Ltd.	229
Alcoa Steamship Co. Inc.	235
Alder & Co., Argo Reederei Richard	410
Alexander Shipping Co. Ltd.	87
Alexandria Navigation Co.	354
Allan Black & Co.	229
Alva Steamship Co. Ltd.	164
American Export Lines Inc.	71
American-Hawaiian Steamship Co.	165
American Mail Line	192
American Pioneer Lines	282
American President Lines	286
American South African Line	194
American Trading & Production Corp.	27
"Amsterdam", N. V. Peederij	321
Anchor Line Ltd.	8
Andrew Crawford & Co. Ltd.	113
Andrew Weir Shipping & Trading Co. Ltd.	175
Andros Shipping Co. Ltd.	214
Anglo Saxon Petroleum Co. Ltd.	195
Argentine Merchant Ships	352
Argo Rederei Richard Alder & Co.	410
Armement Deppe, Soc. Anonyme.	375
Armement L. Hermans, Société Anonyme.	336
Ascot Shipping Co. Ltd.	49

Asiatic Steam Navigation Co. Ltd.	144
Associated Humber Lines	207
Athel Line Ltd.	264
Atlantic Refining Co.	39
Atlantic Steam Navigation Co. Ltd.	290
Australian Steamships Pty. Ltd.	225
Australasian United Steam Nav. Co. Ltd.	104
Aviation and Shipping Co. Ltd.	49
Aznar, Navier, Soc. Anonima.	383

B

Bank Line	175
Barber Steam Ship Line Inc.	129
Batavier Line	344
Belfast Steamships Co. Ltd.	250
Belships Co. Ltd.	404
Ben Line Steamers Ltd.	137
Bergen Line	367
Bharat Line Ltd.	22
Bibby Line	241
Billmeir, J. A.	45
Black Diamond Steamship Corp.	197
Blue "C" Line	402
Blue Funnel Line	288
Blue Star Line	279
Boland and Cornelius	233
Bolton Steam Shipping Co. Ltd.	2
Bombay Steam Navigation Co. Ltd.	248
Booth Steamship Co. Ltd.	25
Booker Line Ltd.	181
Bowring, C. T. & Co. Ltd.	38
Branch Lines Ltd.	57
"Brenntag" (Hugo Stinnes)	362
Bristol City Line	61
Britain S.S. Co. Ltd.	14

British and Burmese 7
British and Continental S.S. Co. Ltd. 227
B. and I. Line (British & Irish S.P. Co. Ltd.) .. 297
British and South American S.N. Co. Ltd. .. 109
British Channel Islands Shipping Co. Ltd. .. 208
British Electricity Authority 273
British India Steam Navigation Co. Ltd. .. 105
British Phosphates Commissioners 5
British Railways 173
British Tankers Co. Ltd. 284
Brocklebank, Thos. and Jno. Ltd. 117
Broken Hill Proprietary Co. Ltd. 114
Broström, Dan-Axel 368, 369, 398
Brövig, Th. 382
Brown & Co., P. 343
Bulk Oil Steamship Co. Ltd. 123
Bull, A. H. & Co. Inc. 69
Bullard, King & Co. Ltd. 198
Buries Markes Ltd. 70
Burke, John Ltd. 295
Burmah Oil Co. (Tankers) Ltd. 228
Burnett Steamship Co. Ltd. 75
Burns and Laird Lines Ltd. 278
Burns Philp & Co. Ltd. 66

C

Cairn Line of Steamships Ltd. 280
California Oil Co. 31
California Transport Corp. 152
Calmar Steamship Corp. 101
Cambay S/S Co. Ltd. 106
Canada Steamship Lines Ltd. 275
Canadian-Australasian Line Ltd. 268
Canadian Department of Transport 303
Canadian Pacific Line Ltd. 155
Canadian National Steamships 283
Carlton S/S Co. Ltd. 106
Cayzer Irvine (Managers) .. 108, 109, 110, 124
Chapman and Willan Ltd. 106
Charente S.S. Co. 121

Charlton Steam Shipping Co. 215
Chellew Navigation Co. Ltd. 16
China Mutual Steam Navigation Co. Ltd. .. 288
China Navigation Co. Ltd. 11
Chine Shipping Co. Ltd. 276
Cities Service Oil Co. 238
City Line Ltd. 203
Clan Line Steamers Ltd. 108
Clarke Steamship Co. Ltd. 163
Clive Shipping Co. Ltd. 185
Clunies Shipping Co. 157
Clyde Shipping Co. Ltd. 10
Coast Lines Ltd. 32
Coast Steamships Ltd. 243
Coastal Tankers Ltd. 256
Cockerline, W. H. & Co. Ltd. 245
Coe, S. Wm. & Co. Ltd. 220
"Cofrunna" 395
Commercial Cable Co. 138
Common Bros. Ltd. 91
Compagnie de Navigation Cyprien Fabre .. 429
Compagnie de Navigation Fraissinet .. 419
Compagnie de Navigation Paquet 324
Compagnie des Bateaux à Vapeur du Nord .. 381
Compagnie des Messageries Maritimes .. 314
Compagnie France-Navigation S.A. 408
Compagnie Générale Transatlantique .. 428
Compagnie Maritime Belge (Lloyd Royal) .. 373
Compagnie Maritime Congolaise 374
Compagnie Maritime des Chargeurs Réunis .. 390
Compagnie Nantaise des Chargeurs de l'Ouest 371
Companhia Colonial de Navegação 386
Companhia Nacional de Navegação 311
Compania Arrendataria del Monopolio de
    Petroleos S.A. 328
Compañia de Navigacion Cristobal S.A. .. 405
Compañia Frutero Valencia de Nav. S.A.
    "Cofrunna" 395
Compañia Sud-Americana de Vapores .. 427
Compañia Trasatlántica 312

Compañia Trasmediterranea	391
Constantine Lines Ltd.	267
Constantine Steamship Line Ltd.	267
Constants Ltd.	90
Continental Line Transport Ferry Service	290
Continental S.S. Co. Ltd.	240
Coolham S.S. Co. Ltd.	23
Cooper, Wm. & Sons Ltd.	169
Coppack Bros. & Co.	179
Corporacion Peruana de Vapores	372
"Corrado", Società di Navigazione	325
Cory, J. and Sons Ltd.	26
Cory, Wm. and Sons Ltd.	60
Costa, Giacomo, Fu Andrea	402
Counties Ship Management Co. Ltd.	161
"Court Line"	174
Crawford, Andrew & Co. Ltd.	113
Creole Petroleum Co.	55
Cunard Steamship Co. Ltd.	272
Currie Line Ltd.	40

D

Daido Kaiun K.K.	364
Dampfchiffshrts-Gesellschaft "Neptun"	365
Dansk-Fransk Dampskib. Akties. Det.	420
Deep Sea Tankers Ltd.	156
De La Rama Steamship Co. Inc.	160
Delmas-Vieljeux, Société Navale	433
Delta Line	222
Denholm, J. and J. Ltd.	93
Denholm Line Steamers	262
Dominion Shipping Co. Ltd.	79
Donaldson Atlantic Line Ltd.	42
Donaldson Line Ltd.	42
Dornoch Shipping Co. Ltd.	59
Duncan, J. T. & Co. Ltd.	4
Dundee, Perth & London Shipping Co. Ltd.	257
Dunlop, Thos. and Sons	15

E

Eagle Oil & Shipping Co. Ltd.	68

East Asiatic	376
Eastern and Australian Steamship Co. Ltd.	12
Eastern Gas and Fuel Assoc.	48
"Elcano", Empresa Nacional	323
Elder Dempster Lines Ltd.	136
Elders and Fyffes Ltd.	166-
Ellermans	201, 202, 203, 204, 205
Ellerman's Wilson Line Ltd.	252
Empresa Nacional "Elcano" S.A.	323
Essberger, John T.	326
Esso Petroleum Co.	55
Esso Shipping Co.	55
Esso Transportation Co.	55
Euxine Shipping Co. Ltd.	153
Evan Thomas Radcliff & Co.	199
Everard, F. E. T. & Sons Ltd.	37

F

Fafalios (Managers)	96
Farrell Lines Inc.	194
Federal Steam Navigation Co. Ltd.	265
"Ferm", Ångbåts Aktiebolaget	369
Fern Line (Fearnley & Eger)	338
Finland Line (Finska Ång. Aktieb.)	355
Fisher, James & Sons Ltd.	209
Fisher, Joseph & Sons	125
Fishguard & Rosslare Railways & Harbours Co.	246
Fjell Line (Olsen & Ugelstad)	359
Flota Mercante del Estado	352
Forenede Dampskibs Selskab, Det	333
France Fenwick, Wm. & Co. Ltd.	50
Fratelli d'Amico-Armatori, Rome	385
Furness-Houlder Argentine Ltd.	86
Furness, Withy & Co. Ltd.	111, 112

G

Gardner, I. and A. & Co. Ltd.	41
Gaze, A. H.	5
General Steam Navigation Co. Ltd.	29
General Steam Nav. Co. of Greece	409

Gibson, G. & Co. Ltd.	3
Glen Line Ltd.	253
Goldsmith, E. J. & W. Ltd.	277
Gorthon Lines	421
Grace Line Inc.	296
Graig Shipping Co. Ltd.	231
Grand Union (Shipping) Ltd.	186
Grangesberg-Oxelosund Trafikaktiebolaget	350
Great Yarmouth Shipping Co. Ltd.	178
Greek Line	409
Grenehurst Shipping Co.	176
Gross & Sons Ltd.	184
Gulf and South American Steamship Co. Inc.	298
Gulf Oil Corp.	211

H

Hadjilias & Co. Ltd.	176
Hahn-Peterson, E...	420
Hadley Shipping Co. Ltd.	189
Hain Steamship Co. Ltd.	17
Halal Shipping Co. Ltd.	261
Haldin & Co. Ltd.	174
Hall Bros. Steamship Co. Ltd.	281
Hall Line Ltd.	201
Hamburg-Amerika Line	412
Hansen, C. K.	407
Harker (Coasters) Ltd.	28
Harries Bros. & Co. Ltd.	188
Harrison, J. & Co. Ltd.	46
Harrison, Thos. and Jas. Ltd.	121
Head Line	34
Headlam & Sons	64
Hector Whaling Co. Ltd...	36
Henderson, P. & Co.	7
Henry, A. F. and MacGregor Ltd.	103
Hermans, L.	336
Heyn, G. and Sons Ltd.	34
Hill, Charles & Sons	61
Hindustan S.S. Co. Ltd.	91
Höegh, Leif & Co., A/S	426

Hogarth Shipping Co. Ltd.	172
Högberg, Eman.	327
Holland Amerika Line	387
Hollandsche Stoomboot Maatschappij. N.V.	399
Holland Steamship Co.	399
Holt, Alfred	288
Holt, John, Line Ltd.	258
Home Lines	417
Hopemount Shipping Co. Ltd.	107
Houlder Bros.	87, 88, 189
Houlder Line Ltd...	88
Hudson Steamship Co. Ltd.	81
Hull Gates Shipping Co. Ltd.	151
Hunting & Son Ltd.	130
Hutchison Moss Line Ltd.	43

I

Iberia Shipping Co. Ltd.	172
Iino Kaiun K.K.	320
Ilwraith, Mc., and McEacharn Ltd.	251
Imperial Oil Shipping Co. Ltd.	122
Independent Tankships Inc.	33
India Steamship Co. Ltd.	85
Indo-China Steam Navigation Co. Ltd.	242
Irish Bay Line	140
Irish Lights	307
Irish Shipping Ltd.	162
Irving, T. G. Ltd.	62
Isbrandtsen Co. Inc.	193
Isle of Man Steam Packet Co. Ltd.	271
Isthmian Steamship Co.	148
Italian Line..	424
"Italia", Soc. per Azioni di Nav.	424

J

Jacobs, J. I. and Co. Ltd.	170
Jahre, Anders	340
Jamaica Banana Producers' S.S. Co. Ltd.	291
Japan Mail Line	370
Java-China-Paketvaart Lijnen, N.V. Konink.	322

Johnson Line	353
Jones, R. W. & Co.	135
Jugoslav Line	430

K

"K" S.S. Co. Ltd.	23
Kawasaki Kisen K.K.	348
Kaye ,Son & Co. Ltd.	23
Kelly, J. Ltd.	126
Kelvin Shipping Co. Ltd... ..	172
Keystone Shipping Co. Ltd. ..	219
Khedival Mail Line	315
King Line Ltd.	168
Klaveness & Co. A/S	337
Knutsen O.A.S., Knut	360
Kohlen-Import U. Poseidon ..	363
Koninklijke Hollandsche Lloyd ..	389
Koninklijke Java-China-Paketvaart Lijnen, N.V.	322
Koninklijke Nederlandsche Stoombt-Maatj. N.V.	356
Koninklijke Paketvaart Maatj. N.V. ..	400
Koninklijke Rotterdamsche Lloyd, N.V.	310
Kyle Shipping Co. Ltd.	116
Kyriakides Shipping Co. Ltd. ..	221

L

Lambert Bros. Ltd.	58, 59
Lamport and Holt Line	289
Larrinaga Line	127
Lauritzen, J.	347
Lauro Armatore, Achille	432
Leeds Shipping Co. Ltd.	260
Lenaghan, Henry P. and Sons Ltd. ..	140
Liverpool and N. Wales Steamship Co. Ltd. ..	134
Lighthouses 301, 304, 307	
Lloyd Brasileiro Patrimonio Nacional ..	418
Lloyd Triestino, Soc. per Azioni di Nav. ..	416
London and Edinburgh Shipping Co. Ltd. ..	78
London and Rochester Trading Co. Ltd. ..	94
London Overseas Freighters Ltd. ..	161
London Scottish Lines Ltd.	76
Longstaff, Comben & Co. Ltd.	80

Luckenbach Gulf Steamship Co. Inc.	92
Luckenbach Steamship Co. Inc.	92
Lykes Bros. Steamship Co. Inc... ..	52
Lykes Lines	52
Lyle Shipping Co. Ltd.	139

M

Mac Andrews & Co. Ltd.	147
MacBrayne, D. Ltd.	249
MacGregor, A. F. Henry &, Ltd. ..	103
Maclay and McIntyre Ltd.	200
Maersk Line	351
Manchester Liners..	266
Marine Industries Ltd.	57
Marine Interests Corp.	83
Marine Transport Lines Inc. ..	83
Maritime Shipping and Trading Co. Ltd.	82
Matheson, Jardine & Co.	242
Mathew, I. H. & Son Ltd.	154
Matson Navigation Co.	183
McIlwraith McEacharn Ltd.	251
Mediterranean Lines Inc... ..	417
Mersey Docks and Harbour Board .. 305, 306	
Messageries Maritimes, Compg. des ..	314
Metcalf Motor Coasters Ltd.	292
Mississippi Shipping Co. Inc. ..	222
Mogul Line Ltd.	120
Möller, A. P.	351
Monks, J. S. Ltd.	47
Monroe Bros. Ltd.	116
Mont Ships.	150
Montreal Shipping Co. Ltd.	150
Moor Line Ltd.	53
Moore McCormack Lines Ltd.	217
Moss, H. E. & Co. Tankers (Holdings) Ltd. ..	190
Moss Hutchison Line Ltd.	43
Mowinckels Rederi, A/S J. Ludwig ..	414
Muhammadi Steamship Co.	224
Müller, Wm. H. & Co.	344
Mystic Steamship Division	48

N

Nailsea Shipping Co. Ltd.	.. ..	199
Natal Line	.. ..	198
National Benzole Co. Ltd.	.. ..	218
Navale Caennaise, Société	..	345
Navigation & Coal Trade Co. Ltd.	..	164
Navigazione Alta Italia	.. ..	431
Nederland Line	.. ..	401
"Nederland" N.V. Stoomv. Maatj.	..	401
Nederlandsch-Amerikannache Stoomv. Maatj.		387
"Neptun", Dampfchifffahrts-Gesellschaft		365
New Zealand Shipping Co. Ltd.	..	143
Nievelt, van, Goudriaan & Co's.	..	394
Nippon Suisan K.K.	.. ..	319
Nippon Yusen K.K.	.. ..	370
Norddeutscher Lloyd Bremen	..	377
"Norden", A/S Dampskibsselskabet	..	343
Nordenfjeldske Dampskibsselskab, Det		342
Nordström & Co. oy., AB.R.	..	366
Norske Amerikalinje A/S, Den	..	397
North American Shipping & Trading Co. Inc.		133
North Coast Steam Navigation Co. Ltd.		247
North of Scotland and Orkney and Shetland Steam Navigation Co. Ltd.	..	146
North Shipping Co. Ltd.	..	259
North Thames Gas Board	..	118
Northern Lighthouse Board	..	304
Northern Steam Ship Co. Ltd.	..	226
Norwood Steamship Co.	..	158
Nourse, James Ltd.	..	212
Nouvelle Compagnie Havraise Peninsl. de Nav.		334

O

Ocean Steam Ship Co. Ltd.	..	288
Oceanic Steamship Corporation	..	183
Oldenburg-Portugiesische..	..	396
Olsen & Co., Fred	..	384
Olsen & Ugelstad	.. ..	359
Ommeren, Phs. Van	..	318
"Oostzee", N.V. Stoomv. Maatj.	..	413

Onesimus Dorey & Sons ..	.. ..	97
Ore Steamship Corporation	.. ..	102
Orient Line ..	.. ..	149
Oriental Trade and Transport Co. Ltd...		56
Orion Shipping & Trading Co. Inc.	..	213
Osaka Shosen K.K.	.. ..	358
Overseas Tankship Corporation	..	30
Overseas Tankship (U.K. Ltd.) ..	..	30

P

P. and O. Steam Navigation Co.	..	13
Pacific, Argentine & Brazil Line..	..	54
Pacific, Atlantic Steamship Co. ..	..	99
Pacific, Far East Line Inc.	..	287
Pacific Steam Navigation Co.	..	142
Pacific Transport Lines Inc.	..	21
Pacific Union Marine Corporation	..	63
Palm Line Ltd.	.. ..	300
Pan American Petroleum and Transport Co.	..	294
Pan Ore Steamship Co. Inc.	..	234
Paterson, N. M. and Sons Ltd. ..	..	18
Pelton Steamship Co. Ltd.	..	95
Peruana de Vapores, Corp.	..	372
Philadelphia Tankers Inc.	..	39
Pocahontas Steamship Co.	..	72
Polarus Steamship Co.	..	131
Polish Ocean Lines	..	392
Poole Shipping Co. Ltd.	..	293
Pope and Talbot Inc.	..	54
Port Line Ltd.	.. ..	269
Port of London Authority (P.L.A.)	..	308
Poseidon (Kohlen-Import U.)	..	363
Power Steamship Co. Ltd.	..	184
Prince Line Ltd.	.. ..	112
Puget Sound Navigation Co.	..	237
Purvis Shipping Co. Ltd. ..	..	49

Q

Quaker Line	.. ..	99
Queen Line	.. ..	15
Queenship Navigation Co. Ltd. ..	..	206

R

Radcliff, E. T., & Co.	199
Raeburn and Verel Ltd.	254
Railway Executive	173
Rankine, Jas. & Son Ltd.	3
Reardon Smith Line	260
Red "R" S.S. Co. Ltd.	185
Redig, Sven	316
Regents Line	186
Reksten, Hilmar	331
Rex, Rederi A/B	329
Rex Shipping Co. Ltd.	176
Richfield Oil Corp.	77
Roberts, Baden H.	16
Roberts, Hugh & Son	259
Robertson, Wm. Shipowners Ltd.	9
Robin Line	132
Robinson, J. & Sons	89
Ropner Shipping Co. Ltd.	293
Royal Fleet Auxiliaries	302
Royal Mail Lines Ltd.	141
Royal Rotterdam Lloyd	310
Runciman & Co. Ltd.	53
Russian Merchant Ships	339

S

S.F.T.P.	313
S.G.T.M.	341
Sabine Transportation Co.	263
Saguenay Terminals Ltd.	73
Sanko Kisen K.K.	330
Scindia S.N. Co. Ltd.	74
Scott, Turnbull & Co. Ltd.	24
Scottish Ore Carriers Ltd.	93
Scottish Shire Line	110
Scottish Tanker Co. Ltd.	124
Seas Shipping Co. Inc.	132
Shaw Savill & Albion Co. Ltd.	180
Sheaf Steam Shipping Co. Ltd.	98
Shell Canadian Tankers Ltd.	156

Ships Finance and Management Co. Ltd.	158
"Sidarma", Soc. Italiana di Armamento	393
Silver Line Ltd.	232
Sinclair Refining Co.	299
Skou, Ove	349
Smith, Christen (Belships)	404
Smith, Reardon Line Ltd.	260
Sociedad Anon. Naviera Aznar	383
Società di Nav. "Corrado"	325
Società Italiana di Armamento "Sidarma"	393
Società per Azioni di Nav., "Adriatica"	415
Società per Azioni di Nav., "Italia"	424
Società per Azioni di Nav., "Tirrenia"	423
Socieà per Azioni di Nav. Lloyd Triestino	416
Société Anonyme Armement Deppe	375
Société Anon. de Gérance et d'Armement	378
Société Française de Transp. Pétroliers	313
Société Générale de Transp. Mari. à Vapeur	341
Société Navale Caennaise	345
Société Navale Delmas-Vieljeux	433
Socony-Vacuum Oil Co. Inc.	35
Souter, W. A. & Co. Ltd.	98
South American Saint Line Ltd.	244
South Atlantic Steamship Line Inc.	223
South Eastern Gas Board	128
Sprague Steamship Co.	236
Stag Line Ltd.	89
Standard Oil Co. of California	19
Standard Vacuum Oil Co.	56
Stanhope Steamship Co. Ltd.	45
States Cargo Carriers Ltd.	213
States Marine Corporation	239
States Steamship Co.	99
Stephen Sutton Ltd.	185
Stephenson Clarke Ltd.	44, 118, 273
Stewart, J. & Co., Shipping Ltd.	100
Stinnes, Hugo	362
Stockholms Rederiaktiebolag Svea	327
Stoomvaart Maatschappij "Oostzee", N.V.	413
Straits Steamship Co. Ltd.	230

14

Strick Line Ltd. 67
Sun Oil Co., U.S.A. 1
Sutherland, B. J. & Co. Ltd. 216
Swedish America Line 379
Swedish East Asiatic Line 380
Swedish Lloyd 422
Swedish Orient (Broström) 398
Swire, John & Sons Ltd. 11
Swiss Shipping Co. 346

T

Tankers, Coastal, Ltd. 256
Tankers Ltd. 264
Temple Steamship Co. Ltd. 58
Thesen's Steamship Co. Ltd. 84
Thomasson Shipping Co. Ltd. 185
Thompson Steamshipping Co. Ltd. .. 187
Thomson, Wm. & Co. Ltd. 137
Tide Water Associated Oil Co. 51
Tirfing Ångf. Aktiebg. 368
Tomlinson Fleet 240
Toyo Kaium K.K. 388
Trader Navigation Co. Ltd. 274
Transmarin A/B 316
Trinidad Corporation 196
Trinity House 301
Turkish Maritime Lines 406
Turnbull, Scott & Co. Ltd. 24
Tyne-Tees Steam Shipping Co. Ltd. .. 115

U

U.S.S.R. 339
Ugelstad, Olsen & 359
Union Castle Line 255
Union Industrielle & Maritime, Soc. .. 357
Union Oil Co. of California 20
Union Steam Ship Co. of New Zealand Ltd. .. 270
Union Steamship Co. of S.A. Ltd. .. 285
United Baltic Corporation Ltd. 177

United British S.S. Co. Ltd. 174
United Fruit Co. 210
United Netherlands Nav. Co. 332
United States Lines (American Pioneer Lines).. 282
United Steamship Company (Denmark) .. 333
United Whalers Ltd. 36
Uskside Shipping Co. 135

V

Van Ommeren 318
Vereenigde Nederlandsche Sheepvaartmaatj. .. 332
Vergottis Ltd. 405

W

Waterman Steamship Corp. 159
Watts, Watts & Co. Ltd. 14
Waverley Overseas Freighters Ltd. .. 96
Weir, Andrew, Ltd. 175
West Hartlepool Steam Nav. Co. Ltd. .. 182
Western Canada Steamship Co. Ltd. .. 65
Westcott & Laurance Line Ltd. 204
Westfal-Larsen & Co. A/S 411
Weyerhaeusen Steamship Co. 119
Whalton Shipping Co. 185
Wilhelmsen, Wilh. 361
Williams, Idwal & Co. Ltd. 231
Williamson & Co. Ltd. 6
Williamstown Shipping Co. Ltd. .. 80
Worms & Cie 312

Y

Yamashita Kisen K.K. 403
Ybarra y Cia 317
Yugoslav Line 430

Z

Zillah Shipping Co. Ltd. 171
Zim Israel Nav. Co. Ltd. 425

15

1   Sun Oil Co., U.S.A.   .... U.S.A.

2   Bolton Steam Shipping Co. Ltd.   .... G.B.

3 { Geo. Gibson & Co. Ltd.   .... G.B.
    Jas. Rankine & Son Ltd.   ....

4   J. T. Duncan & Co. Ltd.   .... G.B.

5 { The British Phosphates Commissioners   .... A.
    A. H. Gaze

6   Williamson & Co. Ltd.   .... H.K.

7 { P. Henderson & Co.   .... G.B.
    British   and Burmese

8   Anchor Line Ltd.   .... G.B.

9   William Robertson Shipowners Ltd.   .... G.B.

10 Clyde Shipping Co. Ltd.   .... G.B.

11 { China Navigation Co. Ltd.   .... G.B.
     John Swire & Sons Ltd. (Managers)

12 The Eastern & Australian Steamship Co. Ltd. G.B.

(For Country of Ownership and Colour Guide see page 68)

HUDDART, PARKER Ltd. A.

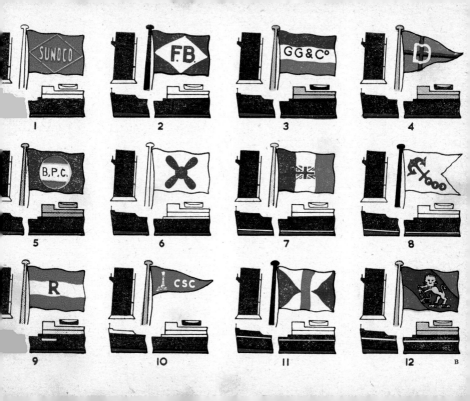

13	P. and O. Steam Navigation Co.	....	....	G.B.

14 { Watts, Watts & Co. Ltd. .... G.B.
     { Britain S.S. Co. Ltd.

15 { Thomas Dunlop & Sons .... G.B.
     { Queen Line

16 { Chellew Navigation Co. Ltd. .... G.B.
     { Baden H. Roberts

17 The Hain Steamship Co. Ltd. .... G.B.

18 N. M. Paterson & Sons Ltd. .... C.

19 Standard Oil Co. of California .... U.S.A.

20 Union Oil Co. of California .... U.S.A.

21 Pacific Transport Lines Inc. .... U.S.A.

22 The Bharat Line Ltd. .... I.

23 { Kaye, Son & Co. Ltd. .... G.B.
     { Coolham S.S. Co. Ltd. and the "K" S.S. Co. Ltd.

24 Turnbull Scott & Co. Ltd. .... G.B.

(For Country of Ownership and Colour Guide see page 68)

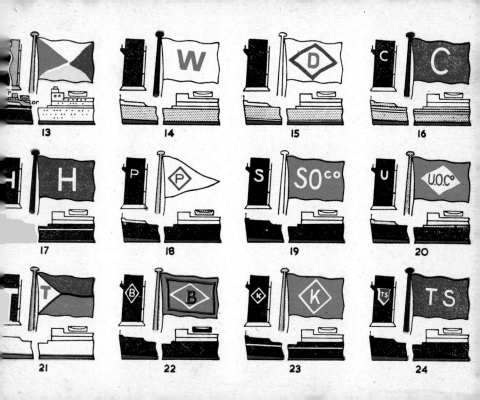

25	The Booth Steamship Co. Ltd.	....	....	G.B.
26	John Cory & Sons Ltd.	....	....	G.B.
27	American Trading and Production Corp.		....	U.S.A.
28	Harker (Coasters) Ltd.	....	....	G.B.
29	The General Steam Navigation Co. Ltd.		....	G.B.
30	{ Overseas Tankship (U.K. Ltd.)	....	....	G.B.
	{ Overseas Tankship Corporation	....	....	U.S.A.
31	The California Oil Co.	....	....	U.S.A.
32	Coast Lines Ltd.	....	....	G.B.
33	Independent Tankships Inc.	....	....	U.S.A.
34	{ G. Heyn & Sons Ltd.	....	....	G.B.
	{ Head Line			
35	Socony-Vacuum Oil Co. Inc.	....	....	U.S.A.
36	{ United Whalers Ltd.	....	....	G.B.
	{ The Hector Whaling Co. Ltd.			

(For Country of Ownership and Colour Guide see page 68)

SWORD LINE INC. U.S.A.

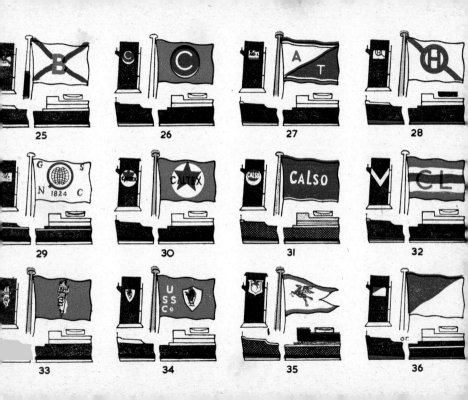

25

26

27

28

29

30

31

32

33

34

35

36

37	F. E. T. Everard & Sons Ltd.	....	....	....	G.B.
38	C. T. Bowring & Co. Ltd.		....	....	G.B.
39	{ The Atlantic Refining Co. Philadelphia Tankers Inc.	....	....	....	U.S.A.
40	Currie Line Ltd.		....	....	G.B.
41	I. and A. Gardner & Co. Ltd.		....	....	G.B.
42	{ Donaldson Atlantic Line Ltd. .... Donaldson Line Ltd. (No Pennant)		....	....	G.B.
43	{ Moss Hutchison Line Ltd. (Spanish Peninsular Fleet) .... Moss Hutchison Line Ltd. (Mediterranean). (Pennant only)				G.B.
44	Stephenson Clarke Ltd.		....	....	G.B.
45	{ Stanhope Steamship Co. Ltd. .... J. A. Billmeir		....	....	G.B.
46	J. and C. Harrison Ltd.		....	....	G.B.
47	John S. Monks Ltd.	....	....	....	G.B.
48	{ Mystic Steamship Division Eastern Gas and Fuel Assoc.		....	....	U.S.A.

(For Country of Ownership and Colour Guide see page 68)

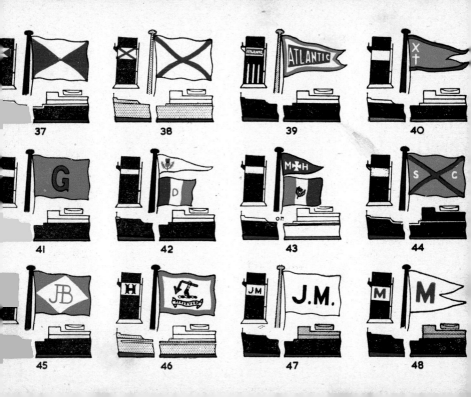

37

38

39

40

41

42

43

44

45

46

47

48

49 {	Aviation & Shipping Co. Ltd.	G.B.
	Ascot Shipping Co. Ltd.	
	Purvis Shipping Co. Ltd.	
50	Wm. France Fenwick & Co. Ltd.	G.B.
51	Tide Water Associated Oil Co.	U.S.A.
52 {	Lykes Bros. Steamship Co. Inc.	U.S.A.
	Lykes Lines	
53 {	Moor Line Ltd.	G.B.
	Runciman & Co. Ltd.	
54 {	Pope & Talbot Inc.	U.S.A.
	Pacific, Argentine and Brazil Line	
55 {	Esso Transportation Co.	G.B.
	Esso Petroleum Co.	G.B.
	Esso Shipping Co.	U.S.A.
	(Creole Petroleum Co.)	U.S.A.
56 {	Standard Vacuum Oil Co.	U.S.A.
	Oriental Trade and Transport Co. Ltd.	C.
57 {	Marine Industries Ltd.	C.
	Branch Lines Ltd.	
58 {	Temple Steamship Co. Ltd.	G.B.
	Lambert Bros. Ltd.	
59 {	The Dornoch Shipping Co. Ltd.	G.B.
	Lambert Bros. Ltd.	
60	Wm. Cory & Son Ltd.	G.B.

(For Country of Ownership and Colour Guide see page 68)

24

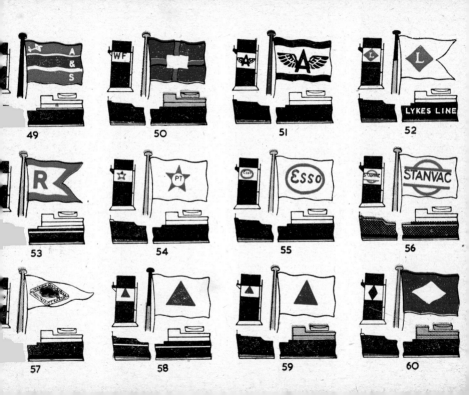

49   50   51   52

53   54   55   56

57   58   59   60

61	Bristol City Line .... Charles Hill & Sons (Managers)	G.B.
62	T. G. Irving Ltd.	G.B.
63	Pacific Union Marine Corporation	H.K.
64	Headlam & Son	G.B.
65	Western Canada Steamship Co. Ltd.	C.
66	Burns Philp & Co. Ltd.	A.
67	Strick Line Ltd.	G.B.
68	Eagle Oil and Shipping Co. Ltd.	G.B.
69	A. H. Bull & Co. Inc.	U.S.A.
70	Buries Markes Ltd.	G.B.
71	American Export Lines Inc.	U.S.A.
72	Pocahontas Steamship Co.	U.S.A.

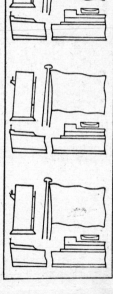

(For Country of Ownership and Colour Guide see page 68)

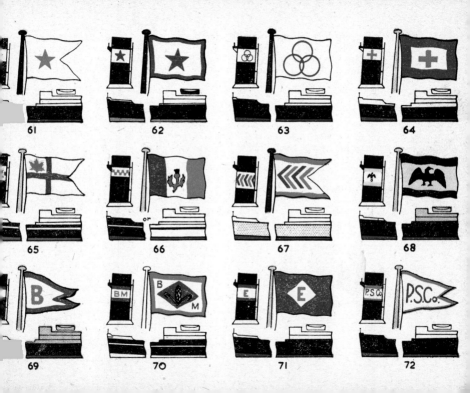

61

62

63

64

65

66

67

68

69

70

71

72

73	Saguenay Terminals Ltd.	....	....	.... C.
74	Scindia S. N. Co. Ltd.	....	....	.... I.
75	Burnett Steamship Co. Ltd.	....	....	.... G.B.
76	London Scottish Lines Ltd.	....	....	.... G.B.
77	Richfield Oil Corporation	....	....	.... U.S.A.
78	London and Edinburgh Shipping Co. Ltd.	....		.... G.B.
79	Dominion Shipping Co. Ltd.	....	....	.... C.

80 { Comben Longstaff & Co. Ltd. .... G.B.
Williamstown Shipping Co. Ltd.

81 Hudson Steamship Co. Ltd. Grey hulls also G.B.

82 The Maritime Shipping and Trading Co. Ltd, G.B.

83 { Marine Transport Lines Inc. .... U.S.A.
Marine Interests Corp.

84 Thesen's Steamship Co. Ltd. .... S.A.

(For Country of Ownership and Colour Guide see page 68)

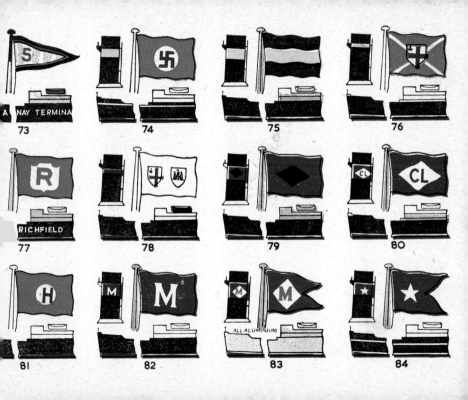

A NAY TERMINA

73

74

75

76

RICHFIELD

77

78

79

80

81

82

ALL ALUMINIUM

83

84

85	India Steamship Co. Ltd.	I.
86	Furness-Holder Argentine Ltd.	G.B.
87	Alexander Shipping Co. Ltd. (Holder Bros.)	G.B.
88	Holder Line Ltd. (Holder Bros.)	G.B.
89	{ Stag Line Ltd. .... { J. Robinson & Sons	G.B.
90	Constants Ltd.	G.B.
91	{ Common Bros. Ltd. .... { Hindustan S.S. Co. Ltd.	G.B.
92	{ Luckenbach Steamship Co. Inc. .... { Luckenbach Gulf Steamship Co. Inc.	U.S.A.
93	Scottish Ore Carriers Ltd. (J. & J. Denholm Ltd.)	G.B.
94	London and Rochester Trading Co. Ltd.	G.B.
95	Pelton Steamship Co. Ltd.	G.B.
96	Waverley Overseas Freighters Ltd. (Managed Fafalios Ltd.)	

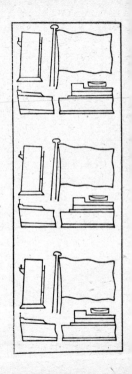

(For Country of Ownership and Colour Guide see page 68)

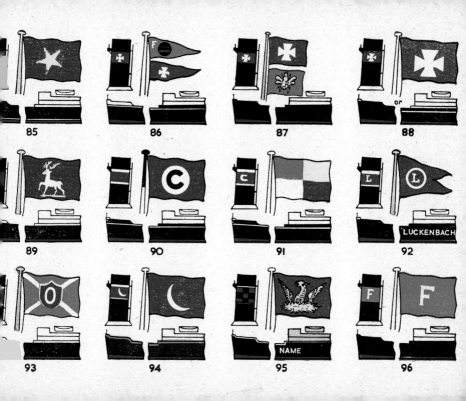

85

86

87

88

89

90

91

92   LUCKENBACH

93

94

95   NAME

96

| 97 | Onesimus Dorey & Sons | .... | .... | .... | G.B. |

98 ⎰ The Sheaf Steam Shipping Co. Ltd. .... G.B.
　　⎱ W. A. Souter & Co. Ltd., Managers

99 ⎧ Pacific—Atlantic Steamship Co. .... U.S.A.
　　⎨ Quaker Line
　　⎩ States Steamship Co. (States Line)

100	John Stewart & Co. Shipping Ltd.	....	....	G.B.
101	Calmar Steamship Corporation	....	....	U.S.A.
102	Ore Steamship Corporation	....	....	U.S.A.
103	A. F. Henry & MacGregor Ltd.	....	....	G.B.

104 The Australasian United Steam Navigation
　　Co. Ltd. .... G.B.

| **105** | British India Steam Navigation Co. Ltd. | .... | G.B. |

106 ⎧ Chapman & Willan Ltd. .... G.B.
　　⎨ The Carlton S/S Co. Ltd.
　　⎩ The Cambay S/S Co. Ltd.

| **107** | Hopemount Shipping Co. Ltd. | .... | .... | G.B. |

108 The Clan Line Steamers Ltd. (Cayzer Irvine—
　　Managers) .... G.B.

(For Country of Ownership and Colour Guide see page 68)

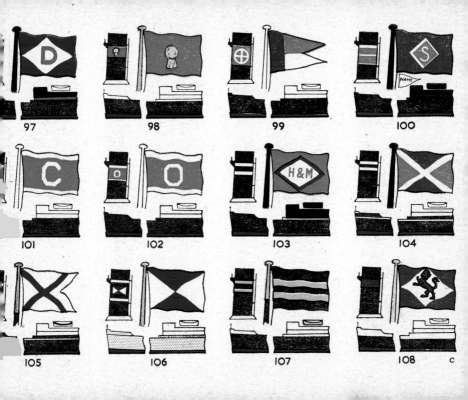

97

98

99

100

101

102

103

104

105

106

107

108

c

109 British and South American S. N. Co. Ltd. (Cayzer Irvine—Managers) .... G.B.

110 The Scottish Shire Line (Cayzer Irvine— Managers) .... G.B.

111 Furness, Withy & Co. Ltd. .... G.B.

112 Prince Line Ltd. (Furness Withy & Co. Ltd.) G.B.

113 Andrew Crawford & Co. Ltd.... .... G.B.

114 The Broken Hill Proprietary Co. Ltd. .... A.

115 Tyne-Tees Steam Shipping Co. Ltd. .... G.B.

116 { Monroe Bros. Ltd. .... G.B.
{ Kyle Shipping Co. Ltd.

117 Thos. and Jno. Brocklebank Ltd. .... G.B.

118 North Thames Gas Board (Stephenson Clarke —Managers) .... G.B.

119 Weyerhaeusen Steamship Co. .... U.S.A.

120 The Mogul Line Ltd. .... I.

(For Country of Ownership and Colour Guide see page 68)

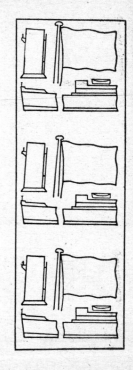

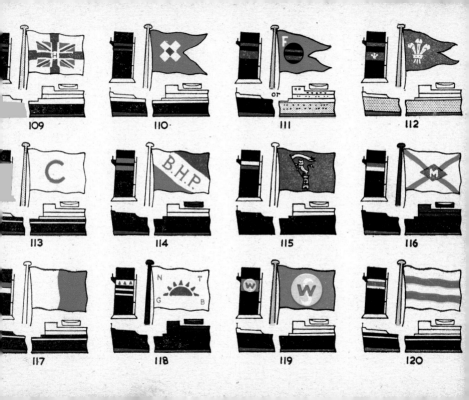

109

110

111

112

113

114

115

116

117

118

119

120

121	Thos. and Jas. Harrison Ltd. Charente S.S. Co.	G.B.
122	Imperial Oil Shipping Co. Ltd.	C.
123	The Bulk Oil Steamship Co. Ltd.	G.B.
124	The Scottish Tanker Co. Ltd. (Cayzer Irvine— Managers)	G.B.
125	Joseph Fisher & Sons	G.B.
126	John Kelly Ltd.	G.B.
127	Larrinaga Line	G.B.
128	South Eastern Gas Board	G.B.
129	Barber Steam Ship Line Inc.	U.S.A.
130	Hunting & Son Ltd.	G.B.
131	Polarus Steamship Co.	U.S.A.
132	Robin Line Seas Shipping Co. Inc.	U.S.A.

(For Country of Ownership and Colour Guide see page 68)

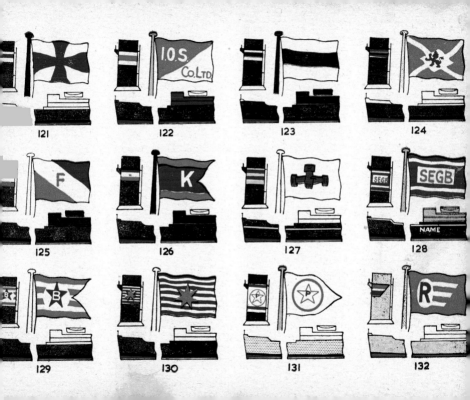

121

122

I.O.S. Co.Ltd.

123

124

125 F

126 K

127

128 SEGB

SEGB

NAME

129 B

130

131

132 R

133 North American Shipping & Trading Co. Inc. U.S.A.

134 The Liverpool and North Wales Steamship
Co. Ltd.   .... G.B.

135 { Richard W. Jones & Co.   .... G.B.
{ Uskside Shipping Co.   ....

136 Elder Dempster Lines Ltd.   .... G.B.

137 { The Ben Line Steamers Ltd.   .... G.B.
{ Wm. Thomson & Co. Ltd.

138 The Commercial Cable Co.   .... G.B.

139 The Lyle Shipping Co. Ltd.   .... G.B.

140 { Henry P. Lenaghan & Sons Ltd.   .... G.B.
{ Irish Bay Lines

141 Royal Mail Lines Ltd. .... G.B.

142 Pacific Steam Navigation Co. .... G.B.

143 The New Zealand Shipping Co. Ltd.   .... G.B.

144 Asiatic Steam Navigation Co. Ltd.   .... G.B.

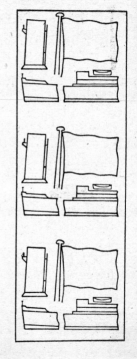

(For Country of Ownership and Colour Guide see page 68)*

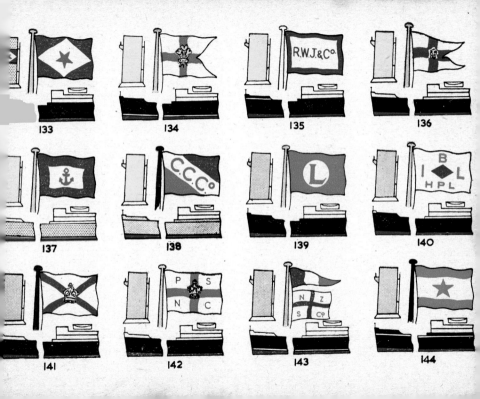

133

134

135

136

137

138

139

140

141

142

143

144

145	Aberdeen and Commonwealth Line	G.B.
146	The North of Scotland and Orkney and Shetland Steam Navigation Co. Ltd.	G.B.
147	Mac Andrews & Co. Ltd.	G.B.
148	Isthmian Steamship Co.	U.S.A.
149	Orient Line	G.B.
150	Montreal Shipping Co. Ltd. .... Mont Ships	C.
151	The Hull Gates Shipping Co. Ltd. ...:	G.B.
152	California Transport Corporation	U.S.A.
153	Euxine Shipping Co. Ltd.	G.B.
154	Acadia Overseas Freighters Ltd. (I. H. Mathew & Son Ltd.)	C.
155	Canadian Pacific Line Ltd.	G.B.
156	Deep Sea Tankers Ltd. (Managers—Shell Canadian Tankers Ltd.	C.

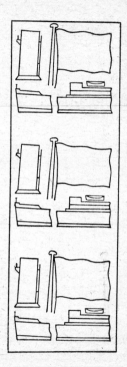

(For Country of Ownership and Colour Guide see page 68)

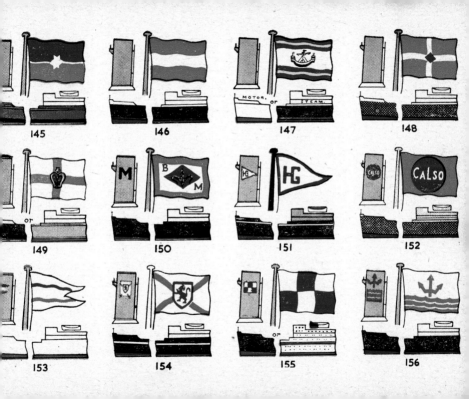

145

146

147

148

149

150

151

152

153

154

155

156

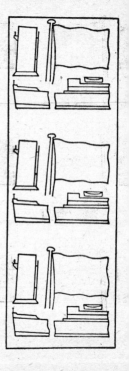

157	Clunies Shipping Co.	G.B.
158 {	Ships Finance and Management Co. Ltd.	G.B.
	Norwood Steamship Co.	
159	Waterman Steamship Corporation	U.S.A.
160	The De La Rama Steamship Co. Inc.	U.S.A.
161 {	London Overseas Freighters Ltd.	G.B.
	Counties Ship Management Co. Ltd.	
162	Irish Shipping Ltd.	E.
163	Clarke Steamship Co. Ltd.	C.
164 {	The Alva Steamship Co. Ltd.	G.B.
	Navigation & Coal Trade Co. Ltd.	G.B.
165	American-Hawaiian Steamship Co.	U.S.A.
166	Elders & Fyffes Ltd.	G.B.
167	The Adelaide Steamship Co. Ltd.	A.
168	King Line Ltd.	G.B.

(For Country of Ownership and Colour Guide see page 68)

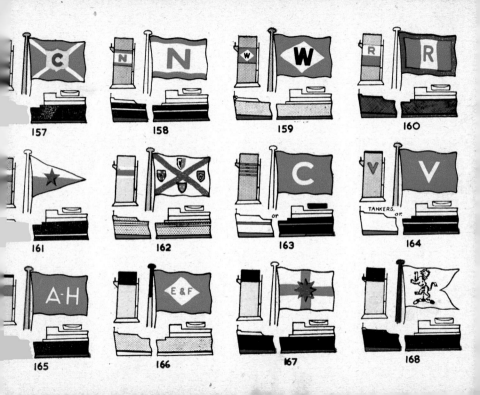

157

158

159

160

161

162

163

164

165

166

167

168

169	William Cooper & Sons Ltd.	....	G.B.
170	John I. Jacobs & Co. Ltd.	....	G.B.
171	Zillah Shipping Co. Ltd.	....	G.B.
172	⎰ The Hogarth Shipping Co. Ltd.		G.B.
	⎨ Iberia Shipping Co. Ltd.		
	⎱ Kelvin Shipping Co. Ltd.		
173	The Railway Executive (British Railways)	....	G.B.
174	⎰ United British S.S. Co. Ltd.		G.B.
	⎱ Haldin & Co. Ltd. ("Court Line")		
175	⎰ The Bank Line		G.B.
	⎱ Andrew Weir Shipping & Trading Co. Ltd.		
176	⎰ Rex Shipping Co. Ltd. (Grenehurst Shipping		
	⎨ Co.)		C.
	⎱ Hadjilias & Co. Ltd.		
177	United Baltic Corporation Ltd.	....	G.B.
178	The Great Yarmouth Shipping Co. Ltd.	....	G.B.
179	Coppack Bros. & Co.	....	G.B.
180	Shaw Savill & Albion Co. Ltd.	....	G.B.

(For Country of Ownership and Colour Guide see page 68)

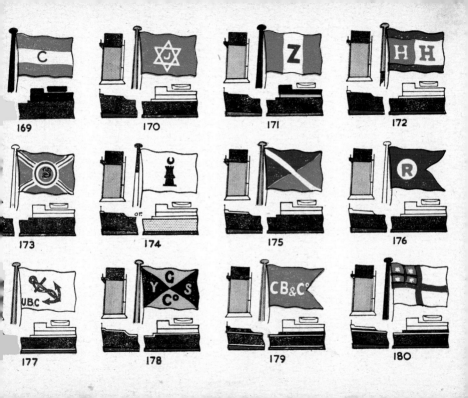

169

170

171

172

173

174 or.

175

176

177

178

179

180

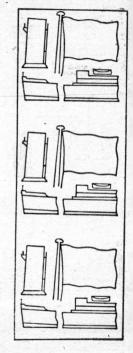

181	Booker Line Ltd.	G.B
182	The West Hartlepool Steam Navigation Co. Ltd.	G.B.
183	Matson Navigation Co. .... Oceanic Steamship Corporation	U.S.A.
184	The Power Steamship Co. Ltd. .... O. Gross & Sons Ltd.—Managers	G.B.
185	Stephen Sutton Ltd. .... The Red "R" S.S. Co. Ltd., The Whalton Shipping Co. Ltd., The Thomasson Shipping Co. Ltd., The Clive Shipping Co. Ltd.	G.B.
186	Grand Union (Shipping) Ltd. .... Regents Line	G.B.
187	The Thompson Steam Shipping Co. Ltd.	G.B.
188	Harries Bros. & Co. Ltd.	G.B.
189	Hadley Shipping Co. Ltd. .... Houlder Bros.	G.B.
190	H. E. Moss & Co's. Tankers (Holdings) Ltd.	G.B.
191	Alaska Steamship Co.	U.S.A.
192	American Mail Line	U.S.A.

(For Country of Ownership and Colour Guide see page 68)

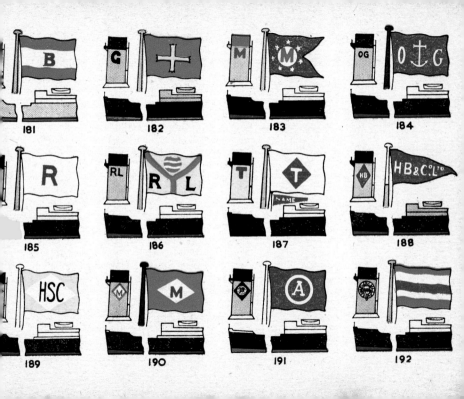

181

182

183

184

185

186

187

188

189

190

191

192

| 193 | Isbrandtsen Co. Inc. | .... | .... | .... | .... | U.S.A. |

194 { Farrell Lines Inc. .... U.S.A.
American South African Line

195 The Anglo Saxon Petroleum Co. Ltd. .... G.B.

196 Trinidad Corporation .... U.S.A.

197 Black Diamond Steamship Corporation .... U.S.A.

198 { The Natal Line .... G.B.
Bullard, King & Co. Ltd.

199 { Evan Thomas Radcliff & Co. .... G.B.
Nailsea Shipping Co. Ltd., E. R. Management
Co. Ltd.

200 Maclay & McIntyre Ltd. .... G.B.

201 Hall Line Ltd. (Ellermans) .... G.B.

202 Ellerman & Bucknall Steamship Co. Ltd. .... G.B.

203 The City Line Ltd. (Ellermans) .... G.B.

204 Westcott & Laurance Line Ltd. (Ellermans) ... G.B.

(For Country of Ownership and Colour Guide see page 68)

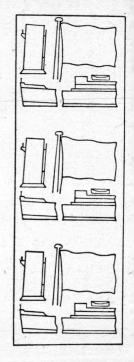

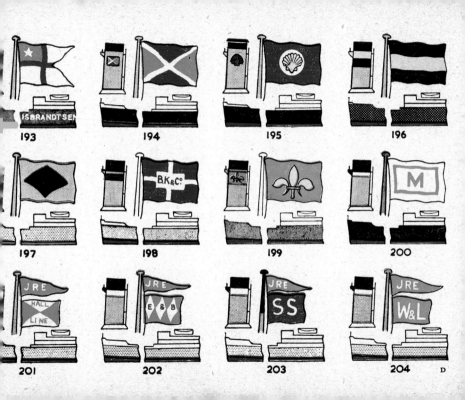

193   194   195   196

197   198   199   200

201   202   203   204   D

205	Ellerman & Papayanni Lines Ltd.	G.B.
206	Queenship Navigation Co. Ltd.	G.B.
207	Associated Humber Lines	G.B.
208	British Channel Islands Shipping Co. Ltd.	G.B.
209	James Fisher & Sons Ltd.	G.B.
210	United Fruit Co.	U.S.A.
211	Gulf Oil Corp.	U.S.A.
212	James Nourse Ltd.	G.B.
213	Orion Shipping & Trading Co. Inc. States Cargo Carriers Ltd.	U.S.A.
214	The Andros Shipping Co. Ltd.	C.
215	The Charlton Steam Shipping Co.	G.B.
216	B. J. Sutherland & Co. Ltd.	G.B.

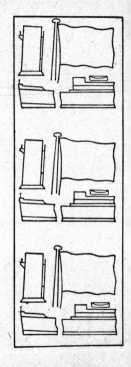

(For Country of Ownership and Colour Guide see page 68)

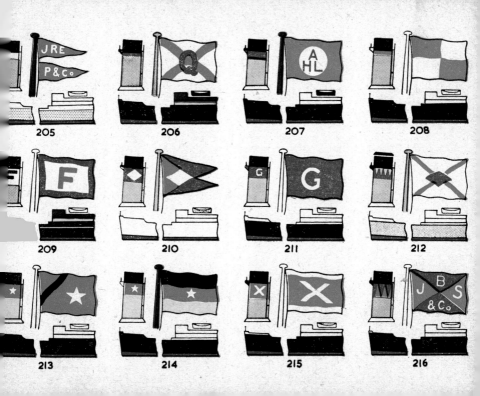

205 206 207 208

209 210 211 212

213 214 215 216

217	Moore McCormack Lines Ltd.	....	....	U.S.A.
218	National Benzole Co. Ltd.	.....	....	G.B.
219	Keystone Shipping Co.	....	....	U.S.A.
220	S. William Coe & Co. Ltd.	....	....	G.B.
221	N. G. Kyriakides Shipping Co. Ltd.	....	....	G.B.
222	Mississippi Shipping Co. Inc. .... Delta Line	....	....	U.S.A.
223	South Atlantic Steamship Line Inc.	....	....	U.S.A.
224	Muhammadi Steamship Co. Ltd.	....	....	P.
225	Australian Steamships Pty. Ltd.	....	....	A.
226	The Northern Steam Ship Co. Ltd.	....	....	N.Z.
227	British and Continental Steamship Co. Ltd.	....	G.B.
228	The Burmah Oil Co. (Tankers) Ltd.	....	G.B.

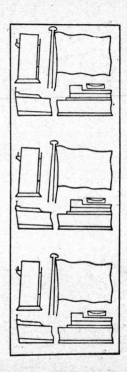

(For Country of Ownership and Colour Guide see page 68)

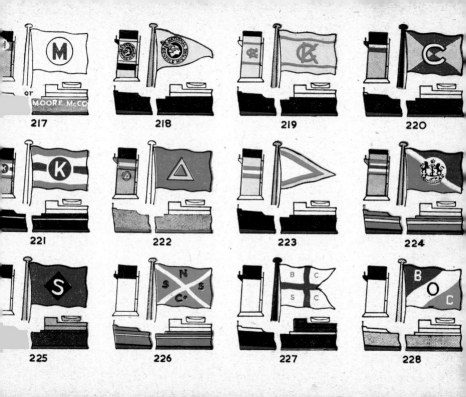

217

or

MOORE McCC...

218

219

220

221

222

223

224

225

226

227

228

229	Albyn Line Ltd. Allan Black & Co.	....	....	....	.... G.B.
230	Straits Steamship Co. Ltd.	....	....	....	M.
231	The Graig Shipping Co. Ltd. Idwal Williams & Co. Ltd.	....	....	....	G.B.
232	Silver Line Ltd.	....	....	....	G.B.
233	Boland & Cornelius	....	....	....	U.S.A.
234	Pan Ore Steamship Co. Inc.	....	....	....	U.S.A.
235	Alcoa Steamship Co. Inc.	....	....	....	U.S.A.
236	Sprague Steamship Co.	....	....	....	U.S.A.
237	Puget Sound Navigation Co.	....	....	....	U.S.A.
238	Cities Service Oil Co.	....	....	....	U.S.A.
239	States Marine Corporation	....	....	....	U.S.A.
240	Tomlinson Fleet.... Continental S.S. Co. Ltd.	....	....	....	U.S.A.

(For Country of Ownership and Colour Guide see page 68)

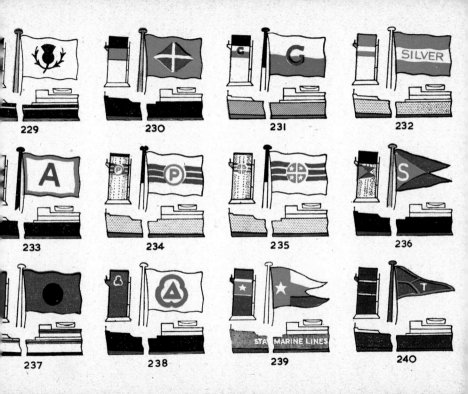

229

230

231

232 SILVER

233 A

234 P P

235

236 S

237

238

239 STAR MARINE LINES

240 T

241 Bibby Line Ltd. .... G.B.

242 { The Indo-China Steam Navigation Co. Ltd. G.B.
Jardine Matheson & Co.—Managers

243 Coast Steamships Ltd. .... A.

244 The South American Saint Line Ltd. .... G.B.

245 W. H. Cockerline & Co. Ltd. .... G.B.

246 Fishguard & Rosslare Railways and Harbours
Co. (British Railways) .... G.B.

247 The North Coast Steam Navigation Co. Ltd. A.

248 The Bombay Steam Navigation Co. Ltd. .... I.

249 David MacBrayne Ltd. .... G.B.

250 Belfast Steamships Co. Ltd. .... G.B.

251 McIlwraith McEacharn Ltd. .... A.

252 Ellerman's Wilson Line Ltd. .... G.B.

(For Country of Ownership and Colour Guide see page 68)

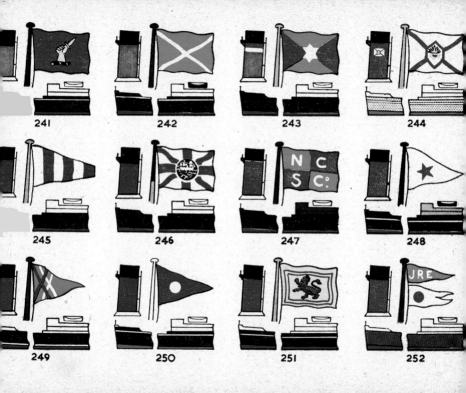

241   242   243   244

245   246   247   248

249   250   251   252

253	Glen Line Ltd.	.... G.B.
254	Raeburn & Verel Ltd.	.... G.B.
255	Union Castle Line (Lavender grey hull)	.... G.B.
256	Coastal Tankers Ltd.	.... G.B.
257	Dundee, Perth & London Shipping Co. Ltd.	G.B.
258	John Holt Line Ltd.	.... G.B.
259	{ The North Shipping Co. Ltd. .... { Hugh Roberts & Son	.... G.B.
260	{ Reardon Smith Line Ltd. .... { The Leeds Shipping Co. Ltd.	.... G.B.
261	The Halal Shipping Co. Ltd.	.... G.B.
262	Denholm Line Steamers	.... G.B.
263	Sabine Transportation Co.	.... U.S.A.
264	{ Athel Line Ltd. .... { Tankers Ltd.	.... G.B.

(For Country of Ownership and Colour Guide see page 68)

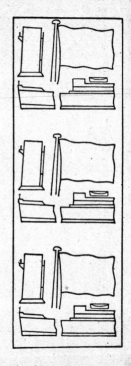

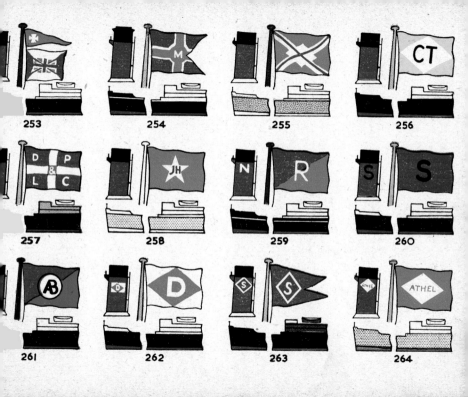

253   254   255   256

257   258   259   260

261   262   263   264

265	Federal Steam Navigation Co. Ltd.	G.B.
266	Manchester Liners	G.B.
267	Jospeh Constantine Steamship Line Ltd. .... Constantine Lines Ltd.	G.B.
268	Canadian-Australasian Line Ltd.	C.
269	Port Line Ltd.	G.B.
270	Union Steam Ship Co. of New Zealand Ltd.	N.Z.
271	The Isle of Man Steam Packet Co. Ltd.	G.B.
272	Cunard Steamship Co. Ltd.	G.B.
273	British Electricity Authority (Managers— Stephenson Clarke Ltd.)	G.B.
274	Trader Navigation Co. Ltd.	G.B.
275	Canada Steamship Lines Ltd.	C.
276	Chine Shipping Co. Ltd.	G.B.

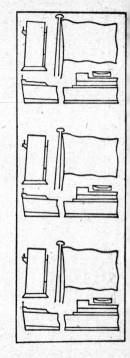

(For Country of Ownership and Colour Guide see page 68)

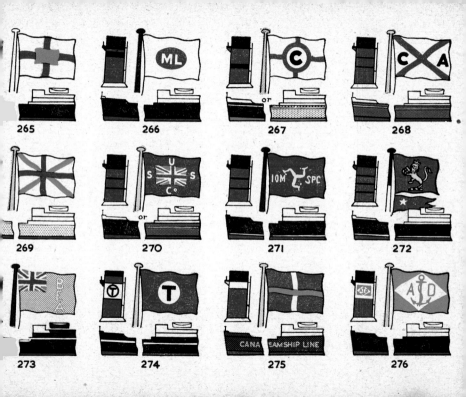

265   266   267   268

269   270   271   272

273   274   275   276

277 E. J. & W. Goldsmith Ltd. .... G.B.

278 Burns and Laird Lines Ltd. .... G.B.

279 Blue Star Line .... G.B.

280 The Cairn Line of Steamships Ltd. .... G.B.

281 Hall Bros. Steamship Co. Ltd. .... G.B.

282 United States Lines (American Pioneer Lines) U.S.A.

283 Canadian National Steamships .... G.B.

284 British Tanker Co. Ltd. .... G.B.

285 Union Steamship Co. of S.A. Ltd. .... S.A.

286 American President Lines .... U.S.A.

287 Pacific Far East Line Inc. .... U.S.A.

288 { The Blue Funnel Line (Alfred Holt) .... G.B.
       Ocean Steam Ship Co. Ltd.
       The China Mutual Steam Navigation Co. Ltd.

(*For Country of Ownership and Colour Guide see page* 68)

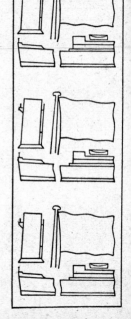

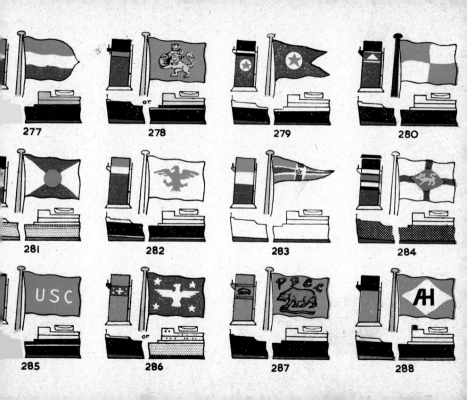

277 278 279 280

281 282 283 284

285 286 287 288

289 Lamport and Holt Line Ltd. .... G.B.

290 { Continental Line Transport Ferry Service .... G.B.
{ Atlantic Steam Navigation Co. Ltd.

291 Jamaica Banana Producers' Steamship Co. Ltd. J.

292 Metcalf Motor Coasters Ltd. .... G.B.

293 { The Ropner Shipping Co. Ltd. .... G.B.
{ The Poole Shipping Co. Ltd.

294 Pan American Petroleum and Transport Co. U.S.A.

295 John Burke Ltd. .... A.

296 Grace Line Inc. .... U.S.A.

297 B. and I. Line (British and Irish Steam E. &
        Packet Co. Ltd.) G.B.

298 Gulf and South American Steamship Co. Inc. U.S.A.

299 Sinclair Refining Co. .... U.S.A.

300 Palm Line Ltd. .... U.S.A. G.B.

(For Country of Ownership and Colour Guide see page 68)

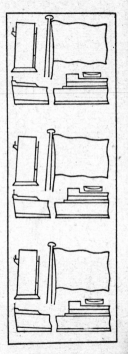

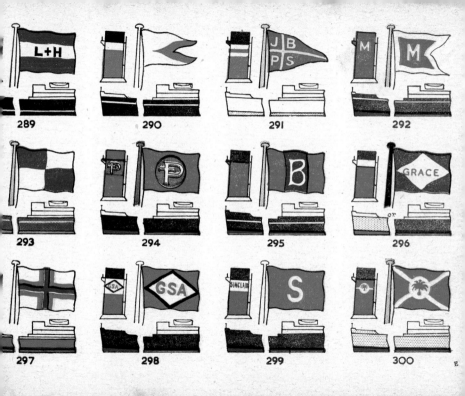

289

290

291

292

293

294

295

296

297

298

299

300

E

301 The Corporation of Trinity House .... G.B.
    (a) House flag or flag of the Elder Brethren
    (b) Ensign—Steam Vessel Service, Pilot Vessels, Lighthouses and Lightvessels
    (c) Cornet worn by Steam vessels and Depots

302 Admiralty (Royal Fleet Auxiliaries)—Ensign only .... G.B.

303 Canadian Department of Transport ships—Ensign only .... C.

304 The Northern Lighthouse Board .... G.B.
    (a) Commissioners House flag
    (b) Ensign
    (c) Commissioners Pendant

305 Mersey Docks and Harbour Board. Marine Dept. Vessels—Ensign only .... G.B.

306 Mersey Docks and Harbour Board. Engineer's Dept. Vessels—Ensign only .... G.B.

307 Commissioners of Irish Lights .... E.
    (a) Commissioners House flag
    (b) Ensign
    (c) Pendant

308 Port of London Authority .... G.B.

309 Royal Mail Pendant (Ships carrying mail) .... G.B.

(For Country of Ownership and Colour Guide see page 68)

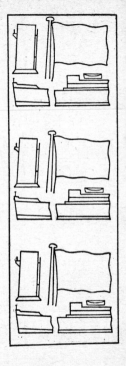

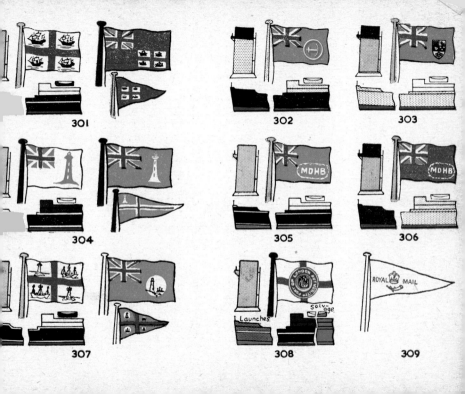

301

302

303

304

305

306

307

308

309

ABBREVIATIONS

The country to which the owning company belongs is indicated by one of the following abbreviations:—

A.	AUSTRALIA	Gm.	GERMANY	P.	PAKISTAN
Ar.	ARGENTINE	H.K.	HONG KONG	Pa.	PANAMA
Bl.	BELGIUM	I.	INDIA	Pd.	POLAND
Bz.	BRAZIL	Is.	ISRAEL	Pg.	PORTUGAL
C.	CANADA	Iy.	ITALY	Pu.	PERU
Ch.	CHILE	J.	JAMAICA	S.A.	SOUTH AFRICA
Dk.	DENMARK	Jp.	JAPAN	Sp.	SPAIN
E.	Republic of IRELAND	Ju.	JUGOSLAVIA	Sw.	SWEDEN
Eg.	EGYPT	Lb.	LIBERIA	Sz.	SWITZERLAND
Fi.	FINLAND	M.	MALAYA	Tk.	TURKEY
Fr.	FRANCE	N.Z.	NEW ZEALAND	Ts.	TRIESTE
G.B.	GREAT BRITAIN	Nd.	NETHERLANDS (HOLLAND)	U.S.A.	United States of AMERICA
Ge.	GREECE	Nr.	NORWAY	U.S.S.R.	RUSSIA

BLACK AND WHITE COLOUR GUIDE

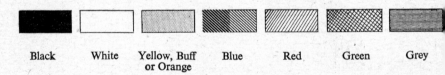

| Black | White | Yellow, Buff or Orange | Blue | Red | Green | Grey |

NATIONAL FLAGS

The gross tonnage of the country is shown by the mast and the number of ships on the right of the flag. The figures are those from *Lloyds Register—Appendix*.

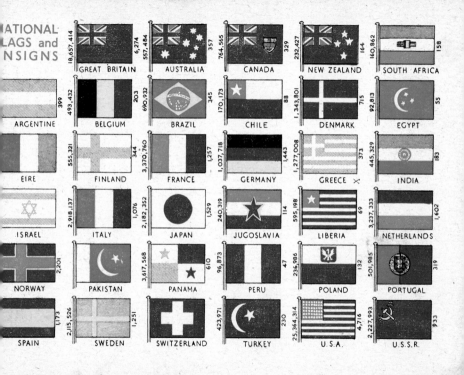

NATIONAL FLAGS and ENSIGNS

Flag	Number	Country
	18,657,414	GREAT BRITAIN
	6,274	
	557,484	AUSTRALIA
	357	
	764,565	CANADA
	329	
	232,427	NEW ZEALAND
	164	
	160,862	SOUTH AFRICA
	158	
	399	ARGENTINE
	493,432	BELGIUM
	203	
	690,932	BRAZIL
	345	
	170,173	CHILE
	88	
	1,343,801	DENMARK
	715	
	92,813	EGYPT
	55	
	555,321	EIRE
	344	FINLAND
	3,370,760	FRANCE
	1,257	
	1,037,718	GERMANY
	1,443	
	1,277,008	GREECE
	373	
	445,329	INDIA
	183	
	2,918,137	ISRAEL
	1,076	ITALY
	2,182,352	JAPAN
	1,529	
	240,319	JUGOSLAVIA
	114	
	595,198	LIBERIA
	69	
	3,237,333	NETHERLANDS
	1,602	
	2,201	NORWAY
	PAKISTAN	
	3,617,568	PANAMA
	610	
	96,873	PERU
	47	
	236,986	POLAND
	132	
	501,985	PORTUGAL
	319	
	1,173	SPAIN
	2,115,526	SWEDEN
	1,251	SWITZERLAND
	423,971	TURKEY
	230	
	25,364,314	U.S.A.
	4,716	
	2,227,093	U.S.S.R.
	933	

310	{Koninklijke Rotterdamsche Lloyd, N.V.	Nd.
	Royal Rotterdam Lloyd	
311	Companhia Nacional de Navegação	Pg.
312	{Worms & Cie. Also	Fr.
	Compania Trasatlantica	Sp.
313	Société Française de Transports Pétroliers (S.F.T.P.)	Fr.
314	Compagnie des Messageries Maritimes	Fr.
315	Khedival Mail Line	Eg.
316	Transmarin, A/B (Sven Redig)	Sw.
317	Ybarra y Cia	Sp.
318	Phs. Van Ommeren N.V.	Nd.
319	Nippon Suisan K.K.	Jp.
320	Iino Kaiun K.K.	Jp.
321	"Amsterdam", N.V. Reederij.	Nd.
322	Koninklijke Java-China-Paketvaart Lijnen N.V.	Nd.
323	Empresa Nacional "Elcano" S.A.	Sp.
324	Compagnie de Navigation Paquet	Fr.
325	"Corrado", Società di Navigazione	Iy.
326	John T. Essberger	Gm.
327	{Stockholms Rederiaktiebolag Svea	
	Eman. Högberg.	Sw.
328	Compañia Arrendataria del Monopolio de Petroleos S.A.	Sp.
329	{Rex, Rederi A/B	
	Ragna Kallstrom	Sw.
330	Sanko Kisen K.K.	Jp.
331	Hilmar Reksten	Nr.
332	{Vereenigde Nederlandsche Scheepvaartmaat-schappij	Nd.
	United Netherlands Navigation Co.	
333	{Forenede Dampskibs Selskab, Det	Dk.
	United S.S.	

(For Country of Ownership and Colour Guide see page 68)

FRENCH RAILWAYS   WORLD TANKER CORP. Lb.

HOLLAND W. AFRICA LINE   REDERIAKTIEBOLAGET IRIS Sw

GUSTAF ERIKSON Fi.   MARTINOLICH CARLO & FIGLIO Ts

S.G. ANDREADIS Ge.   SOC. GERAL DE COMERCIO, INDUSTRIA E TRANSPORTS Pg.

"HANSA" Gm.

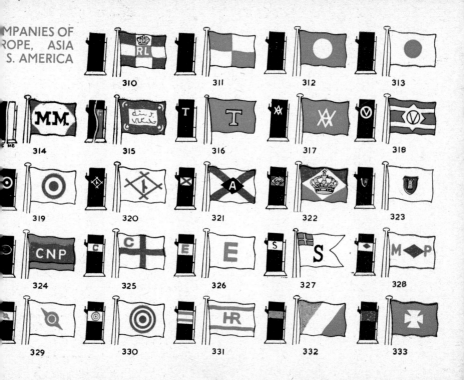

310

311

312

313

314

315

316

317

318

319

320

321

322

323

324

325

326

327

328

329

330

331

332

333

334	Nouvelle Compagnie Havraise Peninsulaire de Navigation	Fr.
335	Aaby's, E. B., Rederi A/S	Nr.
336	Armement L. Hermans, Société Anonyme	Bl.
337	A. F. Klaveness & Co. A/S	Nr.
338	Fern Line (Fearnley & Eger)	Nr.
339	U.S.S.R. Merchant Ships	U.S.S.R.
340	Anders Jahre	Nr.
341	Société Générale de Transports Maritimes à Vapeur S.G.T.M.	Fr.
342	Nordenfjeldske Dampskibsselskab, Det.	Nr.
343	P. Brown & Co. (A/S Dampskibsselskabet "Norden"	Dk.
344	Batavier Line / Wm. H. Müller & Co.	Nd.
345	Société Navale Caennaise	Fr.
346	Swiss Shipping Co.	Sz.
347	J. Lauritzen	Dk.
348	Kawasaki Kisen K.K.	Jp.
349	Ove Skou	Dk.
350	Grängesberg-Oxelösund Trafikaktiebolaget	Sw.
351	Maersk Line (A. P. Möller)	Dk.
352	Flota Mercante del Estado	Ar.
353	Johnson Line	Sw.
354	Alexandria Navigation Co., S.A.E.	Eg.
355	Finland Line / Finska Angfartygs Aktiebolaget	Fi.
356	Koninklijke Nederlandsche Stoomboot-Maatschappij, N.V.	Nd.
357	Union Industrielle & Maritime, Société Française d'Armement	Fr.
358	Osaka Shosen K.K.	Jp.

ADOLF BRATT & CO. Sw.   PER LODDING Nr.

TORM S.S. Co. Dk.   EGON OLDENDORFF Gm.

JACOB KJØDE Nr.   EINAR RASMUSSEN Nr.

S. & D. FAFALIOS Ge.   ALGOT JOHANSSON Fi.

(For Country of Ownership and Colour Guide see page 68)

72

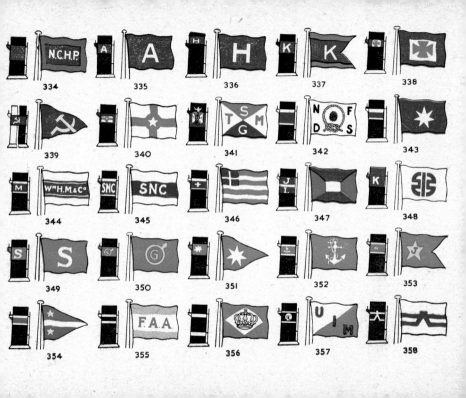

334 335 336 337 338

339 340 341 342 343

344 345 346 347 348

349 350 351 352 353

354 355 356 357 358

359	Fjell Line (Olsen & Ugelstad)	Nr.
360	Knut Knutsen, O.A.S.	Nr.
361	Wilh. Wilhelmsen	Nr.
362	Hugo Stinnes Zweigniederlassung ("Brenntag")	Gm.
363	Poseidon (Kohlen-Import U. Poseidon Schiffahrt A/G)	Gm.
364	Daido Kaiun K.K.	Jp.
365	Dampfchifffahrts-Gesellschaft "Neptun"	Gm.
366	Ab. R. Nordström & Co. Oy.	Fi.
367	Bergen Line / Bergenske Dampskibsselskab, Det.	Nr.
368	Tirfing Angfartygs Aktiebolaget. (Dan-Axel Broström)	Sw.
369	"Ferm" Ångbåts Aktiebolaget. (Dan-Axel Broström)	Sw.
370	Nippon Yusen K.K. / Japan Mail S.S.	Jp.
371	Compagnie Nantaise des Chargeurs de l'Ouest	Fr.
372	Corporacion Peruana de Vapores	Pu.
373	Compagnie Maritime Belge (Lloyd Royal) S.A.	Bl.
374	Compagnie Maritime Congolaise	Bl.
375	Armement Deppe, Société Anonyme.	Bl.
376	Aktieselskabet Det Ostasiatiske Kompagni / East Asiatic Co. Ltd.	Dk.
377	Norddeutscher Lloyd Bremen	Gm.
378	Société Anonyme de Gérance et d'Armement	Fr.
379	Swedish America Line	Sw.
380	Swedish East Asiatic Line	Sw.
381	Compagnie des Bateaux a Vapeur du Nord	Fr.
382	Th. Brøvig	Nr.
383	Naviera Aznar, Sociedad Anonima	Sp.

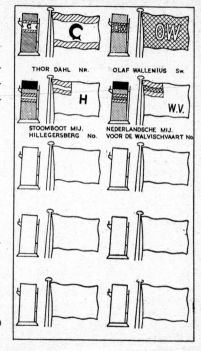

THOR DAHL Nr.   OLAF WALLENIUS Sw.

STOOMBOOT MIJ. HILLEGERSBERG No.   NEDERLANDSCHE MIJ. VOOR DE WALVISCHVAART No.

(For Country of Ownership and Colour Guide see page 68)

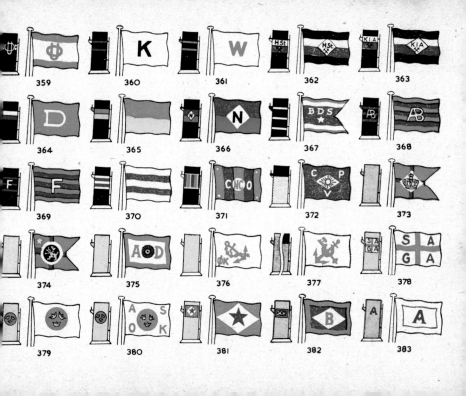

359 360 361 362 363
364 365 366 367 368
369 370 371 372 373
374 375 376 377 378
379 380 381 382 383

384	Fred. Olsen & Co.	Nr.
385	Fratelli d'Amico-Armatori. Rome	It.
386	Compânhia Colonial de Navegacao	Pg.
387	Holland Amerika Line Nederlandsch-Amerikannache Stoomvaart Maatschappij	Nd.
388	Toyo Kiaun K.K.	Jp.
389	Koninklijke Hollandsche Lloyd	Nd.
390	Compagnie Maritime des Chargeurs Reunis	Fr.
391	Compania Trasmediterranea	Sp.
392	Polish Ocean Lines	Pd.
393	Società Italiana di Armamento "Sidarma"	Iy.
394	Van Nievelt, Goudriaan & Co's. Stoomvaart Maatschappij, N.V.	Nd.
395	Compania Frutero Valenciana de Nevega- cion S.A. "Cofruna"	Sp.
396	Oldenburg-Portugiesische Dampfshciffs- Rhederei	Gm.
397	Norske Amerikalinje A/S, Den.	Nr.
398	Swedish Orient Line. (Boström) Svenska Orient Linien	Sw.
399	Hollandsche Stoomboot Maatschappij, N.V. Holland Steamship Co.	Nd.
400	Koninklijke Paketvaart Maatschappij, N.V.	Nd.
401	"Nederland" N.V. Stoomvaart Maatschappij Nederland Line	Nd.
402	Giacomo Costa Fu Andrea Blue "C" Line	Iy.
403	Yamashita Kisen K.K.	Jp
404	Christen Smith & Co. Belships Co. Ltd.	Nr.
405	Compania de Navegacion Cristobal S.A. (Vergottis Ltd.)	Pa.
406	Turkish Maritime Lines	Tk.
407	C. K. Hansen (Donnebrog)	Dk.
408	Compagnie France-Navigation S.A.	Fr.

(*For Country of Ownership and Colour Guide see page* 68)

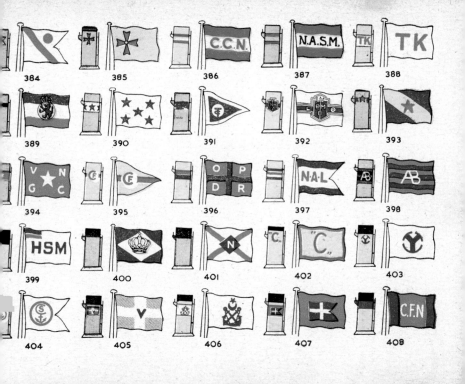

384

385

386 C.C.N.

387 N.A.S.M.

388 TK   TK

389

390

391

392 LCM

393

394 V N G C

395 CF   CF

396 O P D R

397 N·A·L

398 AB   AB

399 HSM

400

401 N

402 "C"   "C"

403

404

405 V

406

407

408 C.F.N

409	Greek Line (General Steam Nav. Co. of Greece)	Gc.
410	Argo Reederei Richard Adler & Co.	Gm.
411	Westfal-Larsen & Co. A/S	Nr.
412	Hamburg-Amerika Line	Gm.
413	Stoomvaart Maatschappij "Oostzee", N.V.	Nd.
414	Mowinckels Rederi, A/S J. Ludwig	Nr.
415	"Adriatica", Società per Azioni di Navigazione	Iy.
416	Lloyd Triestino, Società per Azioni di Navigazione	Iy. & Ts.
417	{ Home Lines	
	Mediterranean Lines Inc.	Iy.
418	Lloyd Brasileiro Patrimonio Nacional	Bz.
419	Compagnie de Navigation Fraissinet	Fr.
420	{ Dansk-Franske Dampskibsselskab. Akties. Det.	Dk.
	E. Hahn-Petersen	
421	Gorthon Lines	Sw.
422	Swedish Lloyd	Sw.
423	"Tirrenia", Società per Azioni di Navigazione	Iy.
424	{ "Italia", Società per Azioni di Navigazione	Iy.
	Italian Line	
425	Zim Israel Navigation Co. Ltd.	Is.
426	Leif Höegh & Co., A/S	Nr.
427	Compañia Sud-Americana de Vapores	Ch.
428	Compagnie Générale Transatlantique	Fr.
429	Compagnie de Navigation Cyprien Fabre	Fr.
430	Jugoslav Line	Ju.
431	Navigazione Alta Italia	Iy.
432	Achille Lauro Armatore	Iy.
433	Société Navale Delmas-Vieljeux	Fr.

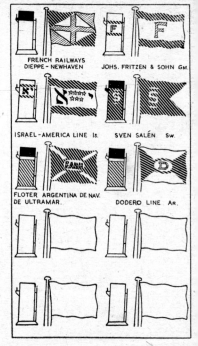

FRENCH RAILWAYS DIEPPE – NEWHAVEN

JOHS. FRITZEN & SOHN Gm.

ISRAEL–AMERICA LINE Is.

SVEN SALÉN Sw.

FLOTER ARGENTINA DE NAV. DE ULTRAMAR.

DODERO LINE Ar.

(For Country of Ownership and Colour Guide see page 68)

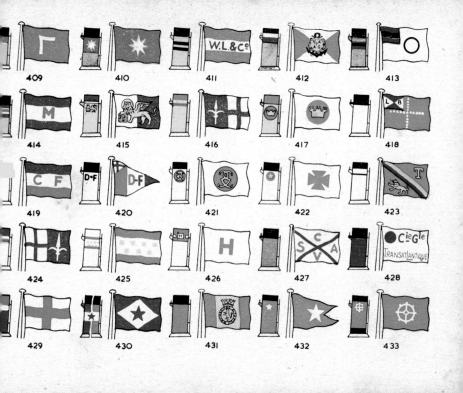

409 410 411 412 413

414 415 416 417 418

419 420 421 422 423

424 425 426 427 428

429 430 431 432 433

ROSS SHIP SERIES

SHIP RECOGNITION—Merchant Ships, by Laurence Dunn .... 12s. 6d. net

SHIP RECOGNITION—Warships, by Laurence Dunn .... 12s. 6d. net

SHIP RECOGNITION—LINERS, by Laurence Dunn .... 12s. 6d. net

YACHTS AND THEIR RECOGNITION, by Adlard Coles and D. Phillips-Birt, A.M.I.N.A. .... 12s. 6d. net

FLAGS, FUNNELS AND HULL COLOURS, by Colin Stewart (Extra Master) .... 6s. 0d. net

SHIPS OF THE ORIENT LINE, by J. H. Isherwood and Colin Stewart (Extra Masters) .... 6s. 0d. net

SHIPS OF THE ROYAL MAIL LINES, by P. Dowden (Lieut., R.N.V.R.) 6s. 0d. net

SAIL. An artist's sketch book, by Michael Lester .... 6s. 0d. net

also

MERCHANT SHIPS—BRITISH BUILT (Fully illustrated with plans and over 200 photographs. A yearly publication) .... 30s. 0d. net

ADLARD COLES LIMITED
(formerly Robert Ross & Co. Ltd.)

WEST PARK ROAD, SOUTHAMPTON